# It's Easy To Play
# Pops 9.

**Wise Publications**
London / New York / Paris / Sydney / Copenhagen / Madrid

Exclusive Distributors:

Music Sales Limited
8/9 Frith Street, London W1V 5TZ, England.

Music Sales Pty Limited
120 Rothschild Avenue, Rosebery, NSW 2018, Australia.

Order No. AM958848
ISBN 0-7119-7898-0
This book © Copyright 1999 by Wise Publications.

Book design by Michael Bell Design.
Cover photographs courtesy of All Action & London Features International.
Compiled by Peter Evans.
Music arranged by Stephen Duro.
Music processed by Allegro Reproductions.

Music Sales' complete catalogue describes thousands of titles and
is available in full colour sections by subject, direct from Music Sales Limited.
Please state your areas of interest and send a cheque/postal order for £1.50 for postage to:
Music Sales Limited, Newmarket Road, Bury St. Edmunds, Suffolk IP33 3YB.

www.internetmusicshop.com

Your Guarantee of Quality:
As publishers, we strive to produce every book to the highest commercial standards.
The music has been freshly engraved and the book has been carefully designed to minimise awkward page turns and to make playing from it a real pleasure.
Particular care has been given to specifying acid-free, neutral-sized paper made from pulps which have not been elemental chlorine bleached.
This pulp is from farmed sustainable forests and was produced with special regard for the environment.
Throughout, the printing and binding have been planned to ensure a sturdy, attractive publication which should give years of enjoyment.
If your copy fails to meet our high standards, please inform us and we will gladly replace it.

Printed in the United Kingdom by
Caligraving Limited, Thetford, Norfolk.

# All I Have To Give

Words & Music by Full Force

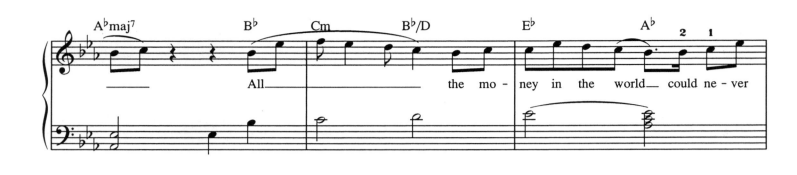

All\_\_\_\_\_ the mo - ney in the world\_\_\_ could ne - ver

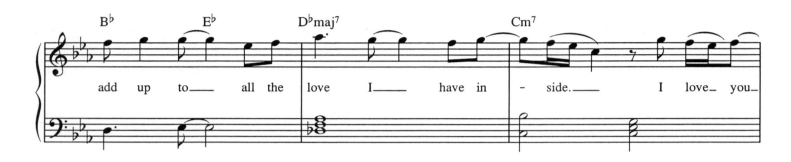

add up to\_\_\_\_ all the love I\_\_\_ have in - side.\_\_\_\_ I love\_ you\_

\_\_ ba - by. And I will give it to\_\_\_ you,\_

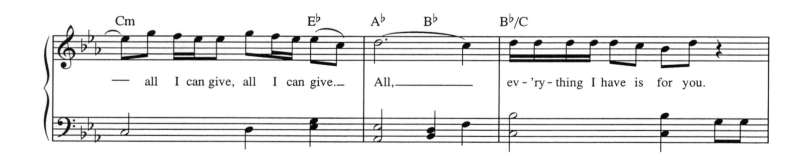

\_\_ all I can give, all I can give.\_\_ All,_____ ev - 'ry-thing I have is for you.

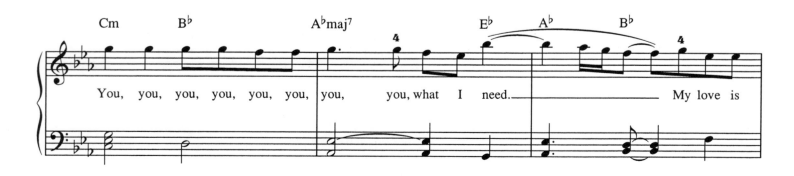

You, you, you, you, you, you, you, you, what I need._____ My love is

*Verse 2:*

When you talk does it seem like he's not
Even listening to a word you say?
That's okay babe, just tell me your problems
I'll try my best to kiss them all away.
Does he leave when you need hin the most?
Does his friends get all your time?
Baby please - I'm on my knees
Praying for the day that you'll be mine.

But my love is all I have to give *etc.*

# I'm Your Angel

Words & Music by R. Kelly

voi - ces when you call___ me, I am your an - gel. And when___ all___

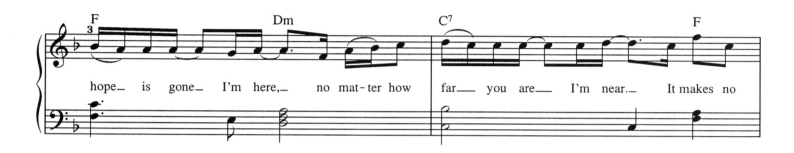

hope___ is gone___ I'm here,___ no mat-ter how far___ you are___ I'm near.___ It makes no

**1.**

dif - fer - ence who you are,___ I am your an - gel.___ I'll be___ your___

**2.**

dif-fer-ence who you are,___ I am your an - gel.___

*Verse 2:*

I saw your teardrops and I hear you crying
All you need is time, seek me and you shall find
You have everything you're still lonely
It don't have to be this way
Let me show you a better day
And then you will see the morning will come
And all of your days will be bright as the sun
So all of your fears, just cast them on me
How can I make you see?

I'll be your cloud *etc.*

# On A Day Like Today

Words & Music by Bryan Adams & Phil Thornalley

whole world could change. The sun's gon-na shine,___ shine through the rain.__ On a

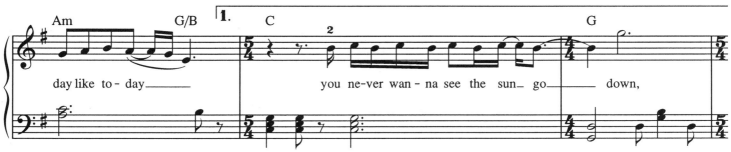

day like to-day___ you ne-ver wan-na see the sun go___ down,

you ne-ver wan-na see the sun go___ down.

no-one com-plains.__ Free to be pure,__ free to be sane.__ On a

day like to-day___ you ne-ver wan-na see the sun go___ down,

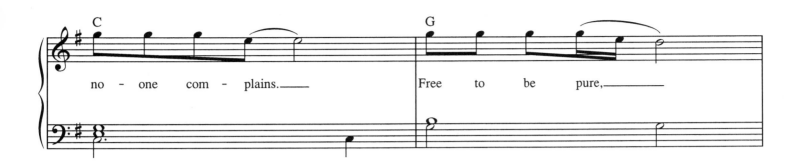

no - one com - plains.____ Free to be pure,____

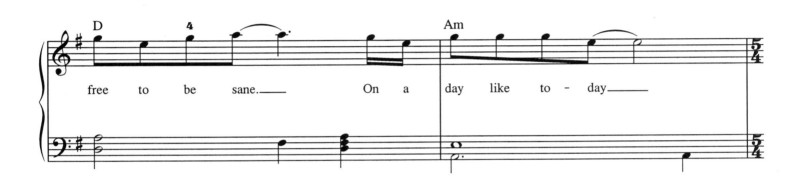

free to be sane.____ On a day like to - day____

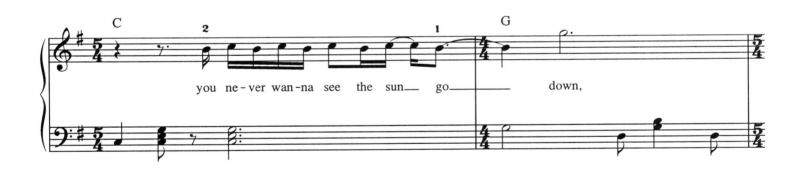

you ne - ver wan-na see the sun__ go_____ down,

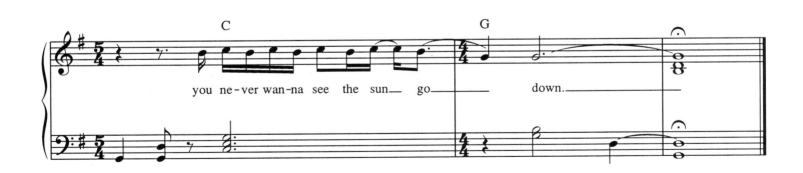

you ne - ver wan-na see the sun__ go_____ down.____

# Perfect Moment

Words & Music by James Marr & Wendy Page

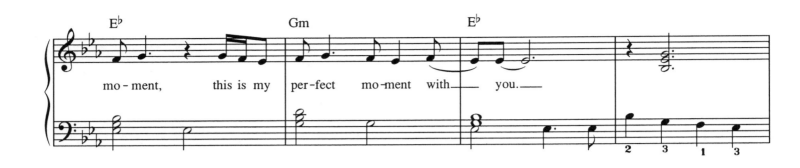

mo - ment, this is my per - fect mo - ment with you.

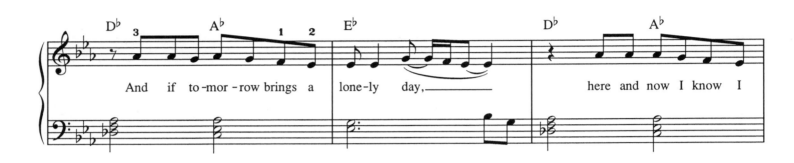

And if to-mor-row brings a lone-ly day, here and now I know I

have - n't lived in vain. No more tears in the rain, and if love ne-ver comes a - gain I can

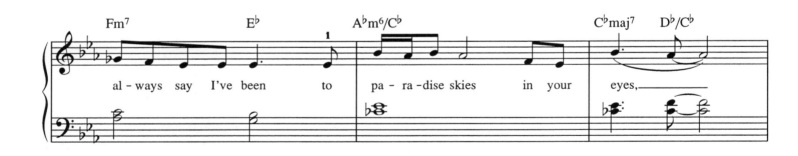

al - ways say I've been to pa - ra-dise skies in your eyes,

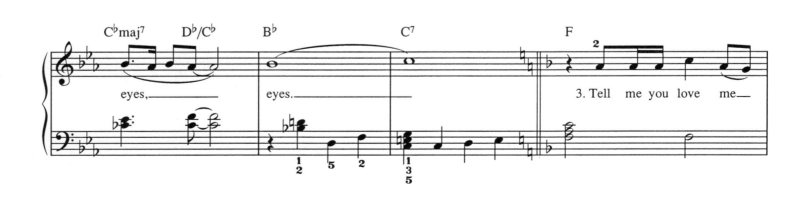

eyes, eyes. 3. Tell me you love me

# Look At Me

*Words & Music by Geri Halliwell, Andy Watkins & Paul Wilson*

**Moderately**

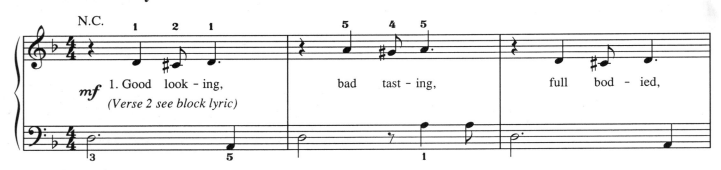

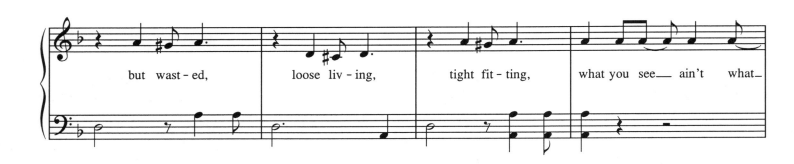

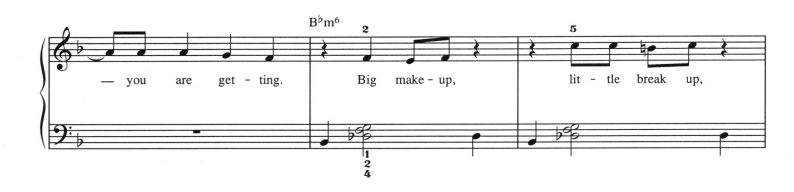

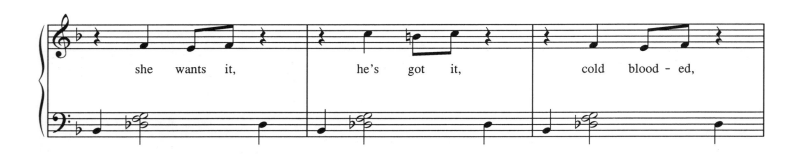

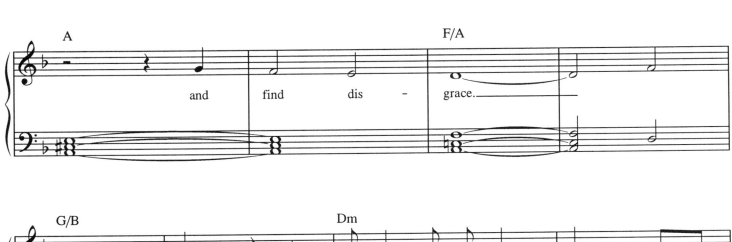

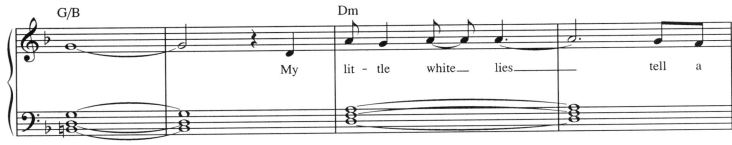

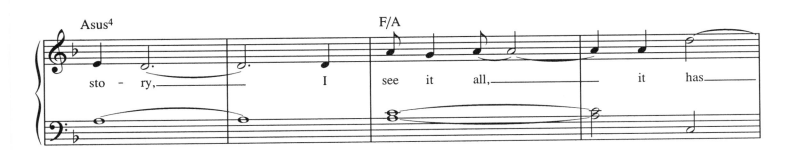

This face is free.    I'm your fan-ta-sy.

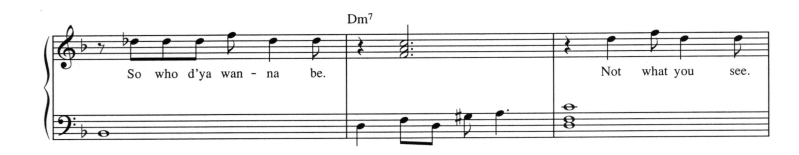

So who d'ya wan-na be.    Not what you see.

I'm a dra-ma queen,

*Repeat ad lib to fade*

if that's your scene.    come on and look at me.

*Verse 2:*

Fake money, real plastic
Stupid cupid, fantastic
Queer thinking, straight talking
What you see ain't what you're getting.
Fast loving, slow moving
No rhythm, but I'm grooving
Old feeling, new beginning
Superficial expectations.

Look at me *etc.*

# She

Words by Herbert Kretzmer
Music by Charles Aznavour

**Moderately slow**

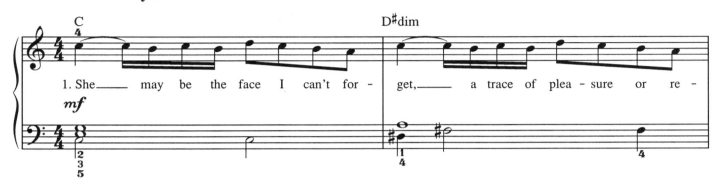

1. She___ may be the face I can't for - get,___ a trace of plea - sure or re -

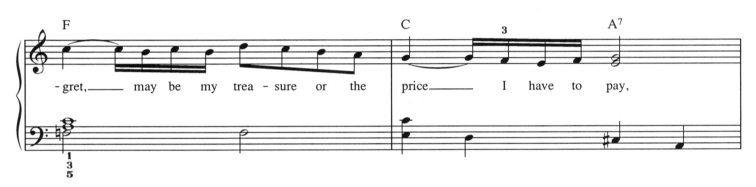

- gret,___ may be my trea - sure or the price___ I have to pay,

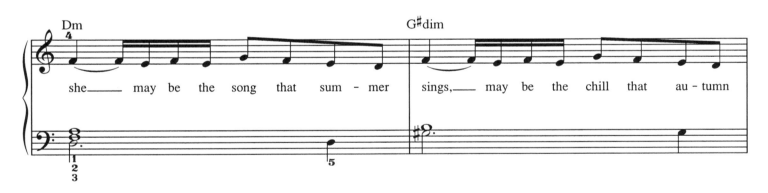

she___ may be the song that sum - mer sings,___ may be the chill that au - tumn

brings, may be a hun -dred diff -'rent things___ with -in the mea-sure of a day.

26

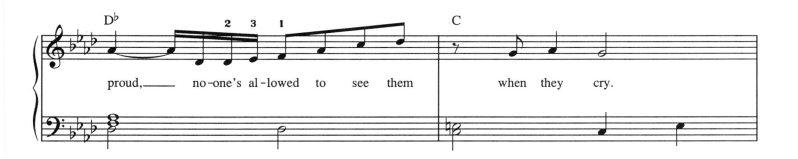

proud,_____ no-one's al-lowed to see them when they cry.

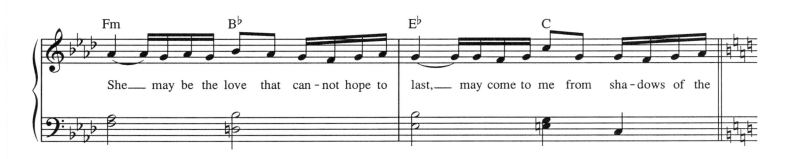

She__ may be the love that can-not hope to last,__ may come to me from sha-dows of the

D.S. al Coda

past_____ that I'll re-mem-ber till the day I die.

CODA

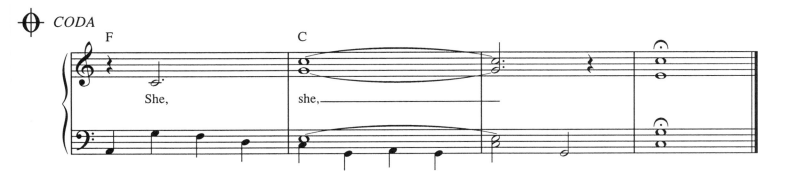

She, she,_____

*Verse 4:*

She may be the reason I survive
The why and wherefore I'm alive
The one I'll care for through the rough and ready years.
Me, I'll take her laughter and her tears
And make them all my souvenirs
For where she goes I've got to be
The meaning of my life is she, she, she.

# Sometimes

Words & Music by Jörgen Elofsson

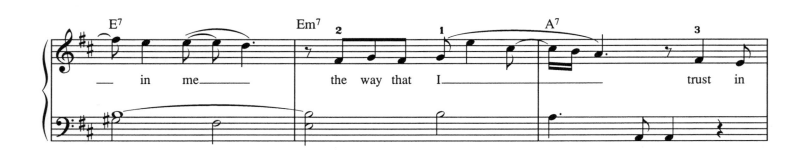

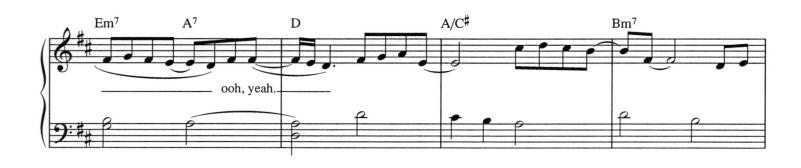

# What Can I Do

Words & Music by Andrea Corr, Caroline Corr, Sharon Corr & Jim Corr

Love me, love me, love love me,

love me, love, love me, love me, love,

love me, love me, love, love me.

*Verse 2:*

There's only so much I can take
And I just got to let it go
And who knows I might feel better
If I don't try and I don't hope.

What can I do...

# When The Going Gets Tough

Words & Music by Wayne Braithwaite, Barry Eastmond, Robert John 'Mutt' Lange & Billy Ocean

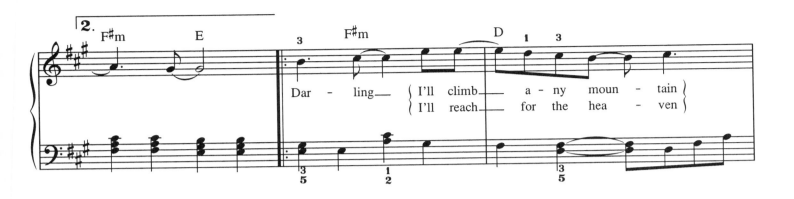

*Verse 3:*

I'm gonna buy me a one way ticket
Nothing's gonna hold me back
Your love's like a soul train coming
And I feel it coming down the track.

(Darling) I'll climb any mountain *etc*

# You Gotta Be

Lyrics & Melody by Des'ree
Music by Ashley Ingram

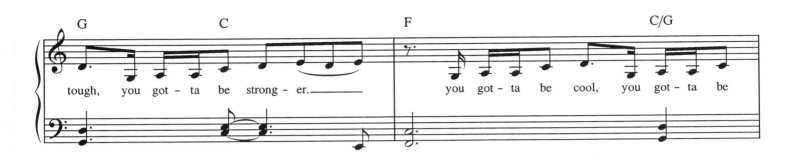

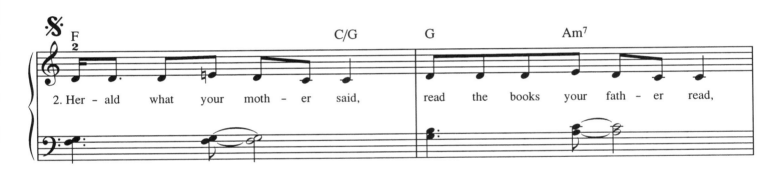

*Verse 3:*

Remember listen as your day unfolds
Challenge what the future holds
Try to keep your head up to the sky
Lovers they may cause you tears
Go ahead release your fears.
My, oh my, hey hey.

# That Don't Impress Me Much

Words & Music by Shania Twain & Robert John "Mutt" Lange

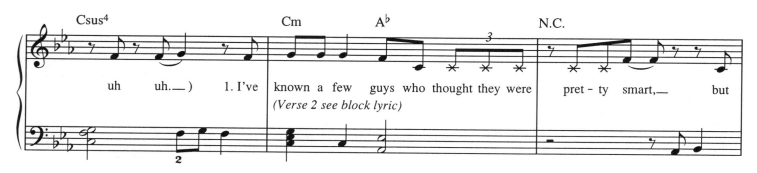

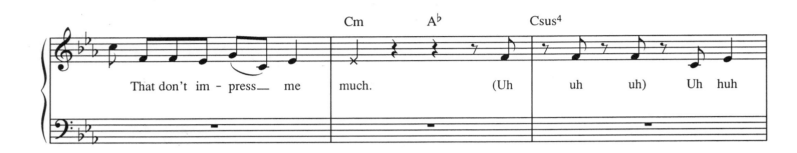

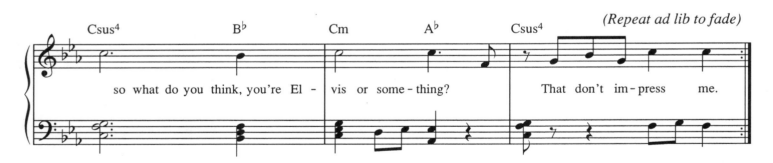

*Verse 2:*

I never knew a guy who carried a mirror in his pocket
And a comb up his sleeve; just in case
And all that extra-hold gel in your hair oughta lock it
'Cause Heaven forbid it should fall outta place.

Ooh, ooh you think you're special
Ooh, ooh you think you're something else
Okay, so you're Brad Pitt.

That don't impress me much *etc*.